OPEN DOORS

BEAUTIFUL WISDOM

LitPrime Solutions
21250 Hawthorne Blvd
Suite 500, Torrance, CA 90503
www.litprime.com
Phone: 1-800-981-9893

Published by LitPrime Solutions   04/22/2022

ISBN: 978-1-955944-81-6(sc)
ISBN: 978-1-955944-82-3(e)

Library of Congress Control Number: 2022907774

CONTENTS

1'st Timothy 6:7 For we brought nothing into this world, and it is certain we can carry nothing out.

THE CURIOSITY OF LIFE

Is life real, or is it a game? have you thought about that, or did you leave it the same? It may be a game that everyone plays, or it might be a rumor that everyone says. Well, we play this game every day? Or will we live by this rumor that everyone says? Will this game end in joy and laughter, or will it end in pain and disaster? Will this rumor go on from year to year, or will it end in sorrow and tears? If this game ends in joy and laughter, we need not worry about what happens after. If this rumor goes on from year to then, we need not worry, and we need no fear. Life could be confusing; it can also be bold; with the happenings in it, there's a story to be told. I'm concentrating hard on this thing called life; the question keeps appearing is it wrong, is it right? Life is full of good and bad things. It's up then down, mysterious, it seems. With all the things we experience and feel, we must ask the question, is life real?

PSALMS 46:10

Be still and know that I am GOD. Therefore, I will be exalted among the heathen, and I will be exalted in the earth.

PSALMS 46:10

FACES

I'm a man of many faces. I've been around to plenty of places. I love and respect all races; do you know who I am? I've been with you since the world was created; I've held your hand when you felt betrayed; I eased the pain when you felt frustrated. Do you know who I am? I taught you to love and only speak the truth. I watched you grow from a child to your youth. In the toughest of times I brought you through, do you know who I am? I blow through your air each day that you rise; I show to you triumph so it can make you wise. I give you my love without any ties. Do you know who I am?

THESE TEARS

These tears that I cry are not just for you. I shed them for the hurt and things I go through. Tears because I miss you; they fall with great pain. Although life goes on, it will never be the same.

No one could understand the depths of my sorrow getting through tonight for a better tomorrow. I may smile, but behind it lies grief; friends come and go; there's just no relief. These tears that I cry are not just for you. I shed them for the hurt and things I go through. If I could trade places to be where you are, I know you're listening, and you're not that far. The hurt has taken over the walls of my pain. Although life goes on, it will never be the same! So many things remind me of you and the unique little things you sometimes like to do. I am strong, but my emotions are weak. These are the times that make me weep. These tears that I cry are not just for you; I shed them for the hurt and thins I go through. I can take the pain! My cup is to top, a switch for my emotions; I'll turn it to stop. My mind is weary; my friends are few; I don't want them around; they haven't a clue. I need to be alone to sort through the grief. I'll smile again; wait and see.

I MUST GO

I must go to the resting place. I'll wait there patiently to see God's face. Do not cry, for my dues are paid. This is the route that God has made.

I left this flesh to get some rest. Be not saddened because God knows best. Don't cry long and be not afraid; just be glad my soul was saved. If you want to meet me once more, knock, and God will open the door. Give him your heart, and let him lead. All over your body, God's blood will bleed. You will be covered, just as I. There is no better way to die. I'll love you always.

A YOUNG GIRL CRY

Please close your eyes and hold your head up towards the sky.

Feel my words as I walk you through a young girl's cry.

Feel my hearts pain as I journey through this path

I am young and decided to leave home. Now that I did, I'm scared and alone. Did you look in my eyes at that last rest stop? I am staring in a place no one else can see. I hope and beg in my heart that someone will rescue me.

I miss my mother, my brother, and my peeps. I often wonder if they miss me. I am growing up fast, taking a gamble with life. He said that he loved me and would make me his wife. Five years later. I'm still in the game; my body is ruined and will never be the same. I can say I'm not in the best health, unrecognizable to myself. I wanted to love but instead got trapped. I'm afraid there's no way for me ever to go back. I was looking for love but soon got played. My dreams and hopes just faded away. I reached out for help and nearly got killed. To the pimps and sex traffickers, it's a laugh or a thrill. Please try to find me. I leave notes all around to get the law enforcement to take their ass down.

Signed by your niece, brother, sister, or friend

WALKING IN MY SHOES

There's something about walking in my shoes; to trade with me, you shouldn't choose. My shoes have been through many miles, not to mention all the different styles; that have come and gone and come back again. They've been through sand, rain, and wind. People laugh, but, I keep on walking as the soles tear more, they start to stalling. I say, come on, shoes, just a few more feet. You bought me through snow, hail, and sleet. You traveled many years throughout my life. You've been good to me like a blade to a knife. I'm growing old in age, so are you, but you took me to places where I expected you to. Out of all the things I may have bought used, you were the best old pair of shoes.

PATHS THAT MEET

An older man had many visions, although he was blind. The things he would see are sure to fascinate you. I have an idea of what you think; if the man is blind, what's fascinating about what he believes he can see? The older man was not only thinking he saw the visions; God genuinely gave him these visions. He smells and looks at beautiful rose gardens, Hills everlasting, flowers, and unspeakable rainfalls. One more thing he sees regularly and the most important is heaven.

The older man couldn't help but talk about these things to whoever would listen. One day the older man was sitting on a bench near a playground; a lady sat on the same court; this lady had severe depression, and after some turmoil in her life, she shut down from society. The man began to speak of his beautiful visions" it seems so natural," the lady thought in her mind, some of the images you could reach out and touch. The lady was more than impressed; she showed an interest, and that's something she gave up on; the lady stated she has dreams of God telling her to go to this playground and sit on this bench. Tears begin to run down the lady's face because she would not allow herself to feel or express anything for years! Due to her extreme depression, it truly can take you over. The lady begins to recite back to the older man all the visions he speaks about pretty rainbows, a beach full of people playing, clouds that are bubbly and blue. The lady can see and feel the images as he describes them. The older man is getting tearful because no one ever wants to listen to him because they don't believe him; they never think of him.

The moral of this story is just because you can't see God does not mean that he's not there. However, you can't see the air; you breathe it in all the time. We live because we breathe the air God gives us; you can't see the gas you put in your car; nevertheless, if a bit of spill, it's the power you can smell it. You can't see it, but it's there. The man and the lady that met each other were no accident; God used one to help the other.

A POT OF GOOD STUFF

I will take some hocks and pinto peas; dice a little onion and garlic leave. Put it on to simmer and cook real slow when my man comes home; that good stuff flow. A pot of love cooked and seasoned to my touch. A warm tub of water says I love you so much. We listen to slow jams as we prepare to eat. I get out the foot soaker for his tired aching feet. My man said baby, dinner smells great. The aroma is so strong that I can hardly wait. He told me the biscuits are golden-like pieces in your life. I'm a blessed man to have you for a wife. I'm sitting on high because of my father up above. A potluck dinner bought a whole lot of love. A meal for five dollars; it's extremely rich in taste. That will keep a smile on my good man's face.

BURNING SECRET

Your secret, you told me, burns in my chest. I weep, and I cry. I never get rest. I toss and turn. I then think of you. I know that you did it! I wish it weren't true. Years have passed, but it hunts me the same; you live life normal while others take the blame. You're secret burns and brings to me stress. I hate you involved me in this mess. How can I fix the damage is deep? I yearn to get just one good night's sleep. I don't understand how this can be; you do dirt, and it falls on me. I rot in here while you see the sun. I feel like running to tell everyone. This secret that burns it hurt my head. I hate to say it, but I wish I were dead. I never thought I'd be in this place, a beautiful life, and what a waste. Look at you just grinning with glee. I'd like to trade places and again be free. You trapped me with promises and lies, untrue—the people who love you if they only knew.

You can go to mass and hail Mary all night; your secret will one day come to light. Everyone will see that you're not real. Then you'll know just how I feel. I hope you sleep well at night; I know Dreams are a pitiful sight. You're fake also, phony, and highly untrue. I still ask God to please forgive you.

CONGRATULATIONS FRIEND

Let me tell you about those so-called friends. They hang around you again and again. They zap! Your energy is like a negative transformation, and; if you think about it, they have no conversation. Friends ney don't come the same; they're full of lies and malicious games. They seem to want everything you've grown instead of going out to get their own. They envy you're may, your home, your car. They despite your freedom because there trapped in a jar. They watch you vigorously with that stupid stare, trying to figure out the next part of your life they can tear. They can't touch you with a ten-foot pole. They've lost their touch; they have no control. You helped them out time and time again; then you say to yourself, there not my friend. They talk and be-little you when you're back is turned a little voice asked will you ever learn? A smile is a frown turned upside down.

You're better off without them following you around. You're highly favored, and they are not. Why do you think they want what you got? You know in your heart they're not genuine. Break them off. It's wade past time. Do that thing and don't look back. Your real true friends will have your back. Smile with ease with no regrets; be done with the first and last time you met. There like chickenpox irritating and itchy; every time you speak, they're cranky and bitchy! Promise yourself to throw the friendship away; don't wait longer. Do this today! Now you have come out of a challenging situation; from me to you, "Congratulations."

CHUCK A CHUCK BOOM

I met a man with a chuck a chuck boom. The car looks like something from out a cartoon. It's classic in its time with a body of rust; when you open the door, Debre and dust. The horn is broken the gas gauge too. How he started that car, I haven't a clue. Don't judge a man by his car or tools; this is a fact from a chuck a chuck boom. He earned his name from years of running. When he turns the corner, you'd hear him coming. Chuck a chuck boom; chuck a chuck boom, then he'd let out this very loud vroom. A collector's item, he's old and antique. The most up respect when he's out on the street. He may be old, but he's plenty of fun; chuck a chuck boom gets the job done. Don't judge a man by his car or his tools. This is a fact from a chuck a chuck boom. His huge toolbox sits deep in the trunk; every bump he hits, they rumble and jump. Anything that breaks, chuck is aware he never goes anywhere unprepared. Don't judge a man by his car or his tools; This is a fact from a chuck a chuck boom. Chuck is tight with every bolt and screw. New cars can't do the things chuck can do. Like a fine wine he's aged with time, he'll always remain a friend of mine.

WHAT GOES AROUND COMES AROUND

I work a job; it's a messed-up place. People will discriminate right in your face. I plead the fifth try not to get involved. If you have a problem, it won't get solved. Bosses are liars and try to make rules; they are a disgrace to society, uncaring fools. They hide their mistakes while shining the light on others. What's done in the dark will come from under the covers. Revealed the truth from an unspoken shame. Look in the mirror, and that's who you blame—singling me out because your position's higher—your nothing but a two-faced backstabbing liar. You give me your word then pretend you forgot; when you fall on your face, I hope you rot. I have no respect for what you've done. I heard you couldn't take it, so you're out on the run. You shouldn't have to run if you know your right; you should stand tall and try to fight. You fight with the position giving you power; that's why you're dismissed this very hour. Funny how life's tables turn. Out of your chaos, I hope you learned. You made this bed, so simply lay down; Remember, what goes around comes back around.

CHECK TO CHECK

I'm so tired of living check to check. I feel like a rope is around my neck, and each day that passes, the rope gets tighter, but I won't give up. I'm a natural-born fighter. My table is stacked and filled with bills; to open them up just gives me chills. Gas, lights, cable, and phone; I wish they all just leave me alone. I can pay some now but not the whole thing; all day long, my telephone rings. When, where, what, and why I'm so frustrated I want to cry.

(Insurance) home, life, and car; my next payday is not that far; there so impatient they just can't wait; they call so I can confirm the date. Now what gets me is they don't stop there; the next person calls, saying your payments are not here. Visa card, Master, Discovery too well. I cut them up because I'm surly through; consolidation companies have run my name; sending all those letters drives me insane. I must owe every bank across the west. I can truly say I have been put through the test. Those credit cards are not for me. If I don't have cash, I'll let it be. I got on my knees and prayed one day for my heavenly father to take them away. Once he did, it taught me the law; I never needed those cards at all! Now I'm not living check to check the rope was removed from off my neck. Now I feel that I can breathe; I might not be rich, but I'm relieved.

DD 911 EQUALS DEATH AND DESTRUCTION

(Attack on our country) Total death and deceit. Suppose you were to leave a letter explaining this day. Death came to visit many citizens, workers children, all unexpected. A private war set up by terrorism to destroy the souls of thousands of people. Innocent people had gone to work daycare with the expectancy to return home. Buildings collapsed as the pain of hollering dust was so thick; you could not escape it. People on the outside watched and yearned to help the inside trapped.

MY POEM DD911

My heart aces and breaks as I play back the tape repeatedly in my mind. A country so powerful had very little time. The invaders had come like a thief in the night; the impact of their destruction was not a good sight. Tourism took lives without signs; we all mourned during this terrible time. Mothers' lost daughters as likewise the same. People held pictures as they yelled out in pain. Children lost parents with no understanding; how could this enemy be so demanding? They didn't give a dam about the lives they took as the planes hit the building; the entire ground shook. The blood of our ancestors was buried in the dust, but we, as Americans, in God, we do trust. The smell of flesh burning, the winds of sorrow; chaos, thinking to get to tomorrow. Our hearts are crushed by a foolish sneak attack. Issues should have been discussed; no! you went behind our backs. DD911, you made our book of shame. You smirk and grin because your dirty work is done; there's no one but you to blame. Now you run and hide, cowardly among your peers. All the money you hold and even you have fears. Next time you see our flag, the stripes and stars that wave. We are Americans, the home of the Braves! To all our fallen soldiers, you've made our book of fame. When the wind blows, it will whistle out your names. We'll set a day aside for prayers and remembrance of you. Well, scream it to the world that you were Americans too. We will love you always! From you, fellow Americans.

A FATHER'S BETRAYAL

The" rageful" nights, the hollering fights!
No good stories about my dad." Mama prayed," but then she stayed
No good stories; yes, this is sad. Many times, I prayed to God to take us
out of this situation, but I felt he didn't listen; it made me more frustrated!

The glare-less stare to a place unknown is where you'd often find me;
it had become my comfort zone, a getaway to help unwind me. Love
and peace she never felt; instead, it was "anger and rage. "I played the
part like it never happened, like an actor on a stage.

I "saw" the love in his eyes; he showed my sister and brother; however
when it gets down to it. He" hated" me and my mother as the years
went on; the abuse continued physical, verbal, and mental. Finally, I
asked a question to the sky. "How could he be so sinful"? My poor
mother, for forty years, waiting to be his bride. All those years of lust
and lies; even so, he had something to hide.

Another son! From a different mother, "Guess that makes him,"
my brother. I looked to the sky and asked the question; did this man
ever love her? Now I have a brother I never met, and this is not his or
my fault. How can my father ever teach; when he can never be taught.
Twenty years of his drinking, weed, and company, staying late at
night. Most "decisions" that he made were very seldom right. I can go
on telling the story; as a result, it makes me tearful. "I choose to walk
away, right now today, to keep my spirit cheerful.

TIME

I am time I wait on no one. You don't scare me; I scare you. Like the yellow, I slip up on you like bitter lemon.

Time, I don't give you time to explain because that's my job. I make you rush, worry and cry. I don't have time to explain why.

Time: It's time to stop comparing me with the devil; I'm too fast for him and won't stoop to his level. You will never see me, but pay attention to my tracks. You'll wonder where the time went and want it back. I don't give in to those puppy sad eyes. I can't hear you, only your cries. I am pro-emotional and can't feel nothing. Come on; people bet your money on something. I make you stay when you know you should have left. I am time; there is nothing else. I caught up with you when you tried to get away. You wondered to yourself where the time went today. I am time in and out with no trace. You will meet me in some part of your day. I am time, and my tracks don't stop; you can turn me off, but I'll remain at the top. It's time for you to accept who and what I am; my possibilities are endless; some call me their friend. I don't have friends because no bargains do I give. I will keep you wondering with no alternatives. I control your life whether you like it or not. You go by my time, and that's all you got. Spend your time wisely because it won't be much to spare. When I strike, you'll know I've been there?

IT'S HER RIGHT

She has strolled through battlefields with souls that apposed her very presence. She beat down the hideous shadows. She once was afraid and felt she was fighting a losing battle. The nerve of her to want you to believe in her when she doesn't believe in herself. She has no mirrors in her house because the reflection would wound her, depress her, and harass her. You said she sounded like she should be on medication. She never told you, but she has been taking twelve pills three times a day for the last three years. She will far succeed in pain, Stress, and worry. Marks peak through with make-up. Hair pieces and wigs covered her scalp, where hair ran long down her back. She told me, "You are my friend nevertheless; with all due respect, it is my right not to fight. I'm so tired of the radiation; it makes me sick. I just never complained. Your fear will pass, and I will become a memory in your mind. The tough times will be fading soon. My destination still lives. You are my best friend; being that it may, it is still my right to give up this fight! One day you will understand; however, it was always my right not to fight!

A NO NAME POEM

This will be a not so sad poem, A not even mad poem; I don't care if you like it or not the poem. This is my poem; whatever you want, make it your poem! I write what I feel, and I think what I write. I Don't care about the media and; its critical hype. It's all the same, and they judge me. The fifth amendment gave me the freedom to speak. I'm writing it down, but I can see it so clear; destruction, government, and homeless people appear. Now, this pulls back from being a sad poem and most defiantly told not to be a mad poem. There are bias, money, theft, the deficit, well-fare prisons, and health. All different issues, yet, the problems are the same.

Lies, truth, a gold digger's game. The things we can't see when the blinds are down. The nose is loud, yet you can't hear the sound.

Some of the biggest thieves wear ties and suits. Some pretend to be poor yet, have crazy loot.

A LETTER

Why have they taken the almighty out of the schools; now, the teenagers are disrespectful and somewhat rude. They do what they want, leaving room to slack; well, I say it's time to bring prayer back. Say a two-minute prayer with the Pledge of a legion. This can be done throughout all the regions. Prayer worked years ago. I read it in a letter, and back in those days, things were better. We didn't hit teachers or blow up the schools; we did what we were told we followed the rules. We had a prayer to start our day; we didn't; lash out when we couldn't get our way. Praying to our almighty could make our children better. I know it for myself because I read it in a letter. Our children are lost, so they turn to destruction. Who has failed them, causing hate and corruption? Prayer should be allowed with no questions asked; they take it away, and kids get too relaxed. They're out of control, smart mouth, and bold. Prayer would be best; tension would be less. Let's bring it back; it's time to act.

THE FATHERLESS CHILD

The child was fatherless because he chose to be. A whole lot of love is what he missed from me. I tried to reach out to be on his side. He wouldn't accept. At least I tried. I have my own money, so I don't need his. Throughout his life, he's been misled. He is told cash is what I am after. Was it worth spending life as a fatherless bastard? The divorce was fatal, affecting my child. Many court battles and numerous papers filed. I took a divorce from my wife, not my son, but in her mind, she thinks she's won. She taught him to hate; look the other way. I will come out with my son one day. (Now he's grown) A fatherless son is what he became. It's not my fault; he rejects his name. I took the blame for many years, and when he hurt, I felt his pain. All I ever wanted was him in my life; all I ever received was broken strife. His mother was determined to keep him to herself, drilling in his head; money and wealth. He has siblings he has never seen, holding grudges in his heart when were from the same team. He was taught hate, and that's not from God. His mother spared the rod and spoiled the child. Now that he's grown and believes I didn't care. I made numerous attempts to try to be there. The door has been slammed right in my face. A father-son relationship becomes a terrible waste. A piece of my spirit will remain in his soul; there are two sides to a story that will one day be told. I am so glad that God is my judge. He taught me to love and let go of the grudge.

PURPLE EVELINA FIELDS

I am passing through the most critical period of my life. Again and again, I have asked myself the question. Why have I failed at so many things? Is it based on selfishness? Love? Am I a fool? Do I not give enough of myself? What is it to love someone and know I have loved them? For the second time in my life, I became jealous, jealous of someone else, and the sad thing about it; was that the person didn't even know me. Do I not have compassion? Have I betrayed anyone? Have I no regrets? I feel so alone. Is there no one in this world for me? Will I ever find love? I went to the hospital today. I visited a friend who is dying. What do you say? To someone that knows they are dying? I see life and death every day. I know so little about one and nothing about the other.

IN DEATHS DOOR-WAY

Have you ever met someone that told you they died and came back? Or they've seen a glimpse of heaven? If the answer is no, consider yourself meeting me. My name is Cindy, nick name Sparkle. I just want to share a story with you. It all is quite an experience; exposure to the other side. I woke up one-day realizing things didn't seem right. My surroundings were dissimilar, altered, and not the same. I didn't hear the birds singing.

My body was at peace; I felt light as a feather; My blood pressure did not bother me; I felt like I could fly, not in a plane. I was not dreaming, people. Things I despised I suddenly liked. It didn't take forty-five minutes to do my hair; nevertheless, somebody had already done it. I was at perfect peace, where I could not recall where I was. I knew I wanted to remain here forever. I understand that no harm could come to me here; I had no fear of anything. There were no regrets. I heard the most beautiful gospel singing that anyone could ever hear. The trees and grass here moved; to the beat of the music, slow and smooth.

When I looked down, I witnessed clouds that were thick and bubbly. Pure as the morning snow but not cold

Thick golden streets miles and miles away, I saw angles everywhere; they were pleasant, enjoyable, and welcoming. There were no old family members or friends reminding me of what I couldn't do. I don't remember my past, and this place is amusing. I feel so good about myself here. I love everyone, and I could feel their love back. I know we all heard the saying, I must have died and gone to heaven. Well, somehow, my body was in-between a debate. I was in that part of my life where a decision had to be made. Somehow, I can feel everyone's heart; it is warm, peace is at hand, and life is grand. The hell I left couldn't pull me back with twenty bulldozers! In the death doorway, I had to choose; that's how things are.

When I stood at the door, I could feel my soul dropping down fast before hitting bottom; I was swept off my feet by perhaps an angel

Scenes of my life flashed before me in five-year segments. At five, I saw myself meeting my father at the Naval Base; he was coming home from the Navy; I had on my pretty pink dress; next, when I was ten, I got chased home from school by bullies. I was so afraid of them that I was fifteen years old and was walking to school the old lady in front of me dropped a fifty-dollar bill. I picked it up and made plans to spend it for myself. In this part of my life, I'm shown that; This was the woman's last money for her medicine, cat food, and groceries. I feel terrible now. I made the wrong decision.

In death's door way I walked through! I can't tell you anymore from this point. Until your day come to walk through the door; if you get the opportunity to walk through.

MOTHER

My Mother is Proud, strong, and loving.
She is caring, giving, and beautiful
She raised six children to be grown and independent
My mother taught me about God
I learned how to go to him and pray
I thank him for life every day. She gave me all I needed to live
There is no greater love than my mother

CRACK BABY CRACK

Another crack baby just freshly, newly born. Born in a world that's prejudiced and torn. Born with a system polluted, not clean. Born to a mother who treated him mean, born with an addiction before taking her first breath. Hooked up to tools, needles, and machines without a hope left. Crack baby crack because you are not to blame; you scream and holler every half hour; your throat is soar and flamed! The odds are against you because your mother didn't care; she ruined your life; just like her own. The outcome isn't fair. She claims she was going to stop, but tomorrow never came. She smoked, sniffed, took a needle, and shot it in your veins! She didn't eat very healthy to give you things you need. As she stands over you crying, her noise starts to bleed! Crack baby crack, and I'll meet you in heaven. You weren't the first to die from your mom; you make crack baby number seven. Seven little lives; so innocent and lost; with your high-risk habit, your babies paid the cost. How could you sleep at night? How could you shut your eyes? I'd imagine that all you hear are all those little cries!!!!!

WAKE UP

He comes around to spend some time just a little while. You're his only woman for the short time that you smile. You don't often smile because soon he has to leave. He must go home to his wife, who he viscously cheats and deceives. You begin to join the cycle; that this is all cool. Don't you forget when it happened to you? O, he said he loves you, and you're his unique jewel. Think back to the day when you broke the golden rule. You started as friends, then more I declare; you both are being selfish, and that isn't fair to the Misses. He told you he would leave her two times, then three and four. All you ever see is him walking out the door. He must return home to the family he once adored. He tells you he has no time for her and treats her pretty mean; you fail to accept the truth that he tells you the same thing. He tells you you're the best and no one can take your place; all your years of nothing were just total waste. He tells you that he hates her and doesn't get along; why is he still with her if nothing were wrong? You need to stop denying this same old tired track. Ask God for forgiveness, then claim your

SON OF DISGUISE

I knew it, son, when I looked in your eyes. I knew you'd be my son of disguise.

    You came with pleasure, heart-ace, and pain, and you have the nerve to brag on your name. I tried so hard to teach you respect, but part of your brain just wouldn't connect. Barley is a man, but you know it all. I stood by your side fall after fall. You disrespect me with your nasty smart mouth. Everything that I taught you, you suddenly doubt. Your father was absent for more than half your life; this made me work harder to do things right. I sacrificed plenty for things you need; in return, your words make my heart bleed! I see my reflection as the water pass by, I'm giving you to God, and I will not cry. I was your first teacher, and I taught you well. Instead, you act like something that burst out of hell. The devil's a liar because I did my best, working doubles and triples so you wouldn't have less. You put up a front to make your papa proud, interrogating my intelligence like I'm on trial. God sits high, and he sees low; you should act your age; how low can you go? God has blessed me with all that I have, and like anything else, this too shall pass. You will need him one day; son, you'll see why God keeps on blessing me. You only pray when you're in need, but one day son, your heart will bleed. God is near, but you push him away. You will scream out his name someday. The sun doesn't set and rise on you, but, in your mind, you think that it do. Your mind has been poisoned and fell in a trap. I will continue to ask God to bring you back.

LOVE THY SELF

You judge me based on credentials, but you know not who I am. You look at me and drop your head as if I'm not good enough to be on your roster. I don't appear wealthy sufficient for you. When you see me, you pretend you don't? You hurt me with your gossip and spread it like a plague. Although you're not cut out to be what you want people to think of you. You live up to other people's standards. You'll never enjoy life because You don't have one. You are dead to your existence. Everything you do must please other people, yet, you look down on me. Some say you have a beautiful personality, but you are bitter, torn, and confused on the inside. So many people think you're all that when in doubt; the scariest thing about it is that many dreams of being like you. Acceptance starts with yourself' denial is the state which must be admitted. I may not have what you have; however, I'm happy with what I possess. Blessed is the man; who is happy for what he has. Inner peace is more remarkable than a pot of money.

KEEPING IT REAL

When I think of my existence, I look up to the high and thank my father, "That's keepnet real. When life's frustration overwhelms the rinse cycle. I will come out squeaky clean. "That's keeping it real. I will remain firm and unbreakable when you wispier and pierce my soul. That's keeping it real. When your sugar, Daddy runs out of things to give. Mines will remain to stand, teaching me to keep it accurate. When the jones that keeps up with the jones is trying to figure out my life. I will remain rich in spirit and prosperity. When I'm down to my last piece of meat, I will not tell you so that you can repeat it. When the voices of friends have come and gone. I will be here for you. With my Almighty father, you're never alone. That's keeping it real.

GREEDY

People of power raised our gas prices, rolling the dice as if we were lifeless. They live in a place called the millionaires club; it's all about them; they don't show us love. Now I'm not angry about their money and fame; it's the average American they continue to drain. I can only put half a tank in my car. We all know that won't take you far. I won't put my furnace above sixty-eight; because when the gas bill comes, that's more on my plate. For one single month, the bill's two- nighty -nine. It's drained my pocket to the very last dime. For dinner last night, I ate peanut butter and jelly; I didn't have meat, but it filled my belly. I Turned on the news; another person got shot. I said to myself; this happens a lot. Another mother cries a part of her dies. So much corruption leads to destruction. How can I make it, I asked myself? I don't have prestige or wealth. My father said live one day at a time, put him first, and I should be fine. I want to live and pay my bills. There're so many obstacles, so many hills. A man can't change the world in four years only. If you think you can, you're misleading and phony.

SPIRIT OF COLORS
AND FRUIT

A young boy and his mother discussed how to teach his more youthful brother his colors. He would have to know and use them throughout his life. The boy's mother always had a unique way of explaining whatever he asked. She would teach other things the same way she first introduced him to his bible. If the boy's mother said seek ye first the kingdom of God, he would finish the prayer by saying, all things would be added to you.

Remember the B's blue, brown and black. Tar on the ground, and its stick's like sap. Brown sugar is sweet, and you can pack it real tight; Blue berry pies as they cool through the night. Green like money could be the route to all evil; olives and lettuce could taste good on sea food. Purple petunias, as they grow out, the ground. Yellow spirits fly without a sound. Red, you right, and orange, you sweet. Dandelions brown as they burn from the heat. White is pure and like cotton to touch. Don't ever forget that I love you so much.

SOFT WHISPERS

I sit by you as you take the last few breaths. So many memories are going through my head. The soft whispers of the last time we talked. I am racing against an unbeatable time that keeps going. I can't imagine life without you. In just a few breaths, I will have no choice. I will forever be filled with the time we spent together. Then, I will grieve the time that is no more. There's a new life that you are about to encounter with Jesus in the dwelling place. The angels must be awaiting your arrival. I hope that there are over ten thousand or more. I know when you get there; the heavy felt burdens would be gone. When the raindrops fall, they can blend with my tears of sorrow. I will weep for only a short while because joy comes tomorrow.

TRICKY LITTLE GAMES

Those tricky little games you always seem to play; will one day turn around and hurt you just the same. I do not wish upon you the bitterness you bought me. Experience is the best teacher; through experience, you will see that love takes time; it's nothing you fix overnight. Sometimes it could be beautiful or piercing like a knife. You let me down with your lying tongue that decided me. I put all the trust I had in you and just looked at how you treated me. You sit there looking stupid with a strange look in your eyes. I think of all the nights I spent trying hard not to cry. I toss and turn, get up, lay down. I don't know what to do. All my sleepless, restless nights. Just because of you. Those tricky little games always brought us down. When I needed you most, you were not around. I wonder how you'll take it; when what you threw gets thrown back at you. Don't think I will take you back; when I hate, I ever knew you—those tricky little games. I wouldn't say I like to keep on mentioning, but something else comes to my attention as I bring this to a closing. I've become a strong woman with a great deal of pride. If you begged too, you were blue to come back to you; I wouldn't even let it phase me.

IN BETWEEN RACES

I went to the mall to look for some clothing; three different people asked whether I may help you. No! after answering them all, they went in their separate directions. The mirror glass across their store revealed faces with frowns, smirks, and grins. Why must you make me feel this within? My money is green and spent like yours, giving me the right to enter this store. O, I see; you can't figure out my race. You feel I don't belong in this place. I continued to shop; very softly; I could hear the salespeople saying, is she black or is she white; her skin completion is kind of light. My blood did boil, and now I'm pretty outraged. I felt like an animal trapped in a cage. I shouted, "I came to shop, not argue about my race." What does it matter the color of my face? The one worker replied that she wasn't talking about me. I explained that it must be raining tacks and nails; they have been sticking me every way but right. Yes, good day to you too. After their insults and racial slurs, it all fiercely got on my nerves. We all should love people from every race, but from every race, some do disgrace us. My mother is black; my father is white. They said we don't judge from one's position or sight. I am the outcome of two great colors, but on forms and applications, I'm labeled as other. My best friend is Chinese, and my man's Hispanic. Did your mouth drop open? Did you start to panic? Race never mattered or tore us apart. Were friends forever in each other's hearts.

I LOVE TO EAT

I love to eat, and that's my one temptation; Yeah, I diet on different occasions—Keil, greens, chicken, and ham. Help me, Lord, I'm in a jam. I partake a desire to eat things, especially cabbage and garlic wings. When I go out, a salad may do, but I can't help to think about some beefy hot stew. On Thanksgiving Day, I must leave the earth. All that good food is what it's worth. The diet drinks are ok, but I can't help but wish. I was sitting at a table eating lobster and fish. You all may laugh, and it's a little bit funny how I relate everything to chicken and honey. Macaroni and cheese with ribs and steak; a three-layered strawberry cream puff cake. I'm a little big with the attention to lose weight. I just don't know what it will take. Shakes, pills and hypnotize won't keep those inches off my thighs. I have tried them, but not for long. My mind starts wondering if I'm not that strong. Mashed potatoes with gravy on top. Roast beef on the side with a nice cold pop. How can I resist such tasteful things; I go back to thinking about ham and greens—potato salad on a hot summer day, a plate for later to send me on my way. Maybe in the future, I'll take my mind off eating. I'll go on a diet without any cheating. You be sure and pray for me; that one day the Lord will set me free.

MY PIANO

When I play my piano, the sound makes love to my soul. Each note that I strike has a different sound. It is so pleasurable to the universe. The sharp and the low keys; were perfectly lined up like soldiers for war. A sound of delegacy is yet bold and definite as it is composure. Each key that I strike reminds me of phases of the yesteryears. My piano is the one thing that brings me back to a lovely place. When I'm angry, I play my piano; when I'm lonely, I play my piano; and when I meditate, I play my piano. The one thing that brings me back to it all. Notes of sadness, cords of good times. You will take up no space in my mind when I play my piano. As I strike the bars from the base keys, it sounds like thunder. My fingers swell as I play a little bit longer. You may love a man or a woman; I love my piano. I once heard there's no greater love than the instruments of the mind—soothing therapy and relaxation for the soul.

THE SILENCE OF TIME

As time keeps ticking, she looks back many years ago at the world compared to now. Her mind comes and goes now and then. She remembers her friends and refuses to believe there gone on to a better place. Some people think she's old. She is brilliant in her secret little way. She peaks at her little watch every couple of seconds as if she was expecting company. With the mind of a Scientist, you should never underestimate her. A present comes in the mail for her; she opens it anxiously to find a large clock that ticked loudly. One thing that she did not like was a watch or clock that she could hear. She loves to gaze at her watch, which does not make a sound—the silence of time.

By mistake only, she knocked the big clock on the floor. When she picked it up, it was still working ok. However, she no longer could hear the ticking. As she looks at her clock, she jumps up quickly to put some bread crumbs on the windowsill for the four birds that fly there every day. Being that it may; she wondered if two of the birds were her two friends that passed away; she giggled and said no because she did not believe in reincarnation. Her head nods as she jerks it to find herself falling to sleep. She wakes up simultaneously; then, she rushes into the same routine that she has followed for years.

LISTEN

If you only listen, you will see just what you're missing. But, unfortunately, your mouth is always flapping, so your hearing starts to be lacking.

Listen with your ears as you watch with your eyes. It will make you a better person. It's sure to make you wise. You will be surprised what you learn to keep quiet. Knowledge would come to you, so why don't you try it. Be open to listening; it's not that hard to do. You would be happy if you did because this would benefit you.

THE FIGHT

I remember my friend and the memories we have. He had war disperse in his heart. His love was gone, and he was my sweetheart. His heart was departing from his other members. His eyes were glaring to a place only he could see. His look on life has become carefree. His only delight was ejecting his gun; the sound of the speed made him run. Often I didn't know where he was going. These changes in him are all mind-blowing. He stares in deep thought with his gun; I know he wouldn't hurt anyone. The system wants to put him in an institution or cage. They said he is dangerous with hell and rage. He's been gone fighting a senseless war, then left all alone like a nasty bed soar. I remember my friend very differently in his life; when he got back, I was to become his wife. He is a man to be loving and gentle; just like that, he's somewhat mental. We both suffered a loss as painful as it gets. In both, our hearts beat a tragic regret.

STILL

I'm still, but it feels like I'm moving very fast!

I want it to be silent, but the quietness is too loud.

At delighted times the sadness is overwhelming

I'm trying to open my mouth, but no words will come out. After that, things will never be the same.

I want to be enraged but can't; I want to jump up and shout. Unfortunately, my feet won't let me move.

I want to relax my mind keeps drifting. I want to accept help, but I'm too proud to ask.

I want to sob, but my pride won't let me. I want revenge, but avenges are not mine. I want to have energy; moreover, I'm restless and edgy. I want to make motions, yet; I'm still like a tree.

NEEDLESS TO SAY

She could be whomever she wants in her mind; it's unfortunate to say she wouldn't mind being anyone but herself. It's clear to see that she's not excited about some events. First, her persuasion to walk paths that don't compliment her, meaning of being here; next, her eyes witnessed chaotic wars that will tear your thoughts apart; finally, a human being or animal should never feel these feelings. Some of her thoughts are brutal but destined for the life that leads her body. Is she a superhero? Maybe. She's less than two worlds apart. In one, she is the mat that keeps it together; in the other world, she has passed all of us on some occasion, helping someone through difficulties. Why can't she reveal who she is? To display it can make her weak and useless; her strength comes from not telling anyone who she is. Could you imagine having a top-secret you can't share with anyone? Her power is in secrecy.

GOLDEN YEARS

He's reached his golden years by far; No more walks; or trips to the bar. His teeth are too big, so they slip out of his mouth. He doesn't like anyone in his house. His knees hurt as they buckle together; he told me it's because of the wet, damp weather. His hair is short with stubby gray whiskers. He can't sit long because his but do blister.

Golden Years
They have come at age ninety-nine; his mind is good as yours and mine. So don't ever boss him or take his choice; You'll never hear the end of his deep raspy voice.

Golden Years
His back is bent slightly, but he still gets around; he and his dog, or as he, say hound. He has a girl which he calls his friend. He treats her nicely, which is better than most men.

MITCH MATCH SOCKS

Where is the other sock? I washed them together; Now, my basket is light as a feather. A few are missing, just disappeared; I can't find them anywhere. Now you understand why I wear two different socks. As long as they're clean, I'm leaving this house. I can't take much time trying to match them the same; The socks are playing me like a silly board game. When I come back in, they suddenly appear. I think I'm going to have a beer.

MR. BO JANGLES

Mr. Bojangles, what can I say? A man of such charisma; a suit and tie kind of man, your shoes are shining so slick; Mr. Bojangles, you're a man for the chicks. When Mr. Bojangles enters a room, women stare at his upkeep and groom. Mr. Bojangles will make the most influential women in the room stare; come to think about it. Mr. Bojangles look good in anything he wears. Or should I say whatever wears him? Mr. Bo jangles, just let me stare; ooh, how you wear your hair. It isn't much that Bojangles can't do; he spreads much love for me and you. Mr. Bojangles won't settle for less; he looks good with his big, broad chest. A man who makes you inhale and hold' he's not shy; he's flashy and bold.

When he passes can't help but see; some possibilities between him and me; Hum Mr. Bogangles every woman's wish. He's better than you're best-tasting dish. When God made man, he made him well. Mr. Bojangles, you kiss and tell; if you don't tell, then I won't tell. Mr. Bojangles, well, well, well!

GRUDGES

How long are you going to hold that grudge? Sooner or later, it will begin to deteriorate your heart and mind. Holding grudges keeps you from reaching your true inspirations in life. Holding grudges keeps your mind on things that are not important. Holding grudges blocks the genuine faith you have in yourself. I freeze up your confidence in God. Holding grudges will keep you in a state of unsureness and confusion. A resentment hinders you and blocks your mind from receiving proper understanding.

MY PRAYER TO GOD

God, I pray you to break every chain and link of fear, low finances, family curses, poor health, and habits.

Please break back biting, confusion, jealousy, envy, bondage, uncertainties, unsureness, thieves, liars; please, God, give us peace from you. May we lift you and glorify you to the fullest. Thank you for your son, Jesus, that died on the cross for our sins. We ask that you cure this mean virus Covid. Please keep us protected from any new virus. Please protect us from any hurt or danger.

Thank you

THE FIVE STAGES OF DEATH

Don't get caught up in the five stages of death. You better do it right now while there's still time left. Tomorrow is not promised, so you better change fast because none of us know how long our lives will last. Imagine lying on your death bed bargaining for time. Is it the last thing you may have on your mind? Yes, I've watched it happen time and time again; people deny death right to the end. They know they must accept it and take what's coming; as they review their lives, they know they are running out of time as; it draws the family nearer. Death is something coming, although it makes us all inferior. Death means the end; no more, all gone. You might have been a person that did not do much wrong. You may be the person that's stuck on your wealth; the five stages of death will take your health. You may show anger, and that will pass soon; You may buy an expensive doctor that can't mend the wound; of the five stages you know are coming. You refuse to believe, and your mind keeps you running. You'll slow down to bargain for time; this can't be bought, so it burdens your mind. You think of other answers, but time is running out. You think of all the damage you have done and try to sort it out.

When it gets down to it, there's not enough time. You never thought it couldn't happen to you; you think you've lost your mind. Of course, it's not your mind you're losing; it's your life, and you're afraid. Finally, however, you must lay down in this bed you made. The five stages of death are no joke; it's for real.

WOUNDS HEALED

Moving on with you is all that is important. I have waited; it seems an eternity for this day to come. Moving on with you, my beginning, and my purpose. My love, we will become one in love; in my heart and soul. I never thought that happiness would revisit my heart, You, and only you, the essential element of my living. You are the part that makes me complete.

The ghost and the demons made me believe love was a good thing for a short while; then came you. Right then and their destinies meet. You have healed the wounds of my heart: no more ghosts or uncertainties. Because of you, we can look forward to our future of greatness. We will jump hurdles; we will jump and climb together. It will be you and me forever. I love you, crave you, and accept you. My heart and soul say I love you.

LIFE OF A CHAIR

Have you ever thought about the life of a chair? All the buts they hold are not fair: big buts, little buts, and huge buts too. No one would believe what a chair goes through. Sitting in your den and to no one do they faze. They are sick and tired, and they all want a raise and not the raise of a rag dusting us down. If it weren't for us, you'd be sitting on the ground, the floor, and the rug, whichever you please. We are something curtail that everyone needs. People sit on us and blow hot air. Kids have accidents; now, is that fair? Now, if we go on strike and keep all you're buts from on us. We might call the coaches and loveseats to come to join us. Now you might look mighty strange typing standing up, standing at the breakfast table drinking from your cup, standing in the movies trying to watch the show. So we thought we'd speak our minds and let the world know.

UNTIL HELL FREEZES OVER

You thought this would be a nicely- nice song; until hell freeze over again, you're wrong.

You've been headstrong your entire life long; just let me sing my country song. You worked my nerves until they were gone. I want to sing a lovely swan song. You and I don't belong Until hell freeze over, leave me alone. All you do is fuss and grown; you're on your own; you're a woman scorned.

Until hell freeze over, shut your blabbermouth, pack your bags and perhaps head south. I'm fed up; and ready to bounce; you drained me down to my last ounce. Sometimes I ask if hell will freeze over; you remind me of a broken recorder.

Repeat line one in that exact order; then pack your things and head to the border.

I'VE NEVER SEEN THE RIGHTEOUS FORSAKEN

Lord, here I call again, another trying day at work. Everything that went wrong, of course, had something to do with me. "My nerves are jumping with fear" because someone almost ran me off the road! This raggedy old car is on its last ride and desperately needs work. Kids are acting up in school; Mark cut his classmates' ponytails off. The gas bill is four hundred ninety-nine dollars. Where will I get the money to pay it?

My best friend is on the phone complaining about her man. My brother stopped by and asked to borrow twenty dollars; "I need that for tomorrow's dinner." Lord, I know you don't like complainers, but I need some help! Sometimes I feel like giving up; I can't help but wonder if I will ever see the light at the end of the tunnel?

GOD RESPONSE

My dear child, I'm pleased you call on me; be humble that you can call on me. Remember that everything that seems wrong is not wrong. If you start to have fear, immediately replace it with faith.

I will clothe you in my entire armor. Your car may be raggedy and old, but ask yourself, didn't it start up and take you to your job? Doctor appointment or destination? Remember three years ago, when you did not have a license to drive and bring more understanding to this situation? Wasn't you that called yourself the bus, train, or uber queen? I sometimes know children act up in school. At least there're in school. When you stated that the gas bill is high, be grateful that you have a home that has gas. You said you didn't know where you would get the money.

Did you forget I'm your almighty father? I own everything on this earth. Did you get so caught up in the daily activities that you forgot how to come to me and pray? Your best friend on the phone is complaining about her man; unless she wants to change things, you certainly can't. Sometimes, my dear, you forget to concentrate on your life, making other people's problems yours. When it seems like you have very little money, I know when someone important in your life needs it for their emergency. I taught you not to worry about what you will eat, drink or wear. When you put me first, I have already taken care of all your needs. Do you have any questions? "No, I don't, but I want to thank you. I love you. Please come and talk to me again, Have your way, lord.

FALCONS

I remember the days I tried to do well with you. You shattered my hopes and desires. You, the one person I thought understood my thoughts and visions. You blind me like a chemical. I made you feel that life without you is impossible; you made me believe in nonexistence. I tried to overlook the remorseful times. You, the constant reminder. I stood up for you when so many others ridiculed your name. You put me down so low; the dirt from the earth thought I was its grandmother. When I ponder you, I think of vultures, a bird of prey. Most birds have free spirits with a song to sing. I will pray for you because you are a falcon.

INNOCENT EYES

Innocent eyes have seen too much in a lifetime; the back has deteriorated with broken blood vessels. Each blink reveals an unwanted memory. The small wrinkles reveal age and secrets. The inside of the eye reveals the pulps that lost their way. The iris flashes short scenes of an unknown path; the sclera is no longer white; it's faded, dull, and yellowish.

Innocent eyes seem jumpy and nervous. Anyone will admit that they've been through wars and tragedy; then they blink another memory of some sad scene. Unfortunately, this is not a fix for an eye doctor.

CORONA

You are small but grew large; you came to our world to show you are in charge. You wreck lives took a thousand souls; continuous test going up to our nose. You shut us down our schools and stores. We couldn't keep up; we soon grew poor. We had to close with no money to pay; worldwide is one sad day! Symptoms spread from place to place; record-high numbers case by case. Stimulus went out to boost our economy. Who do we blame the real democracy? Believe it or not, things started to improve. Corona Virus, you're hateful and cruel. Killin people while taking their strength, charging them guilty as if they're on the bench. You have killed adults, babies, and kids breaking our spirits like branches and twigs. Leave our existence to leave us alone. We want to go back to a place called home. Hospitals are full, so the family can't stay. I don't know if our families' will see another day!

Vaccines and Boosters may slow you down, but we'll fight like hell when you come back around. Body aches, sneezes, can hardly breathe. Fever, headache, I pray that they leave. There are not enough ventilators to get us all through. You attacked us by surprise; we didn't know what to do. So, we'll part here; please let yourself out. You're never welcome to any of our houses!

THE DEVIL KEEPS WATCHING

The devil keeps watching; he wants you to slip. He waits for you anxiously to lose your grip. He visits your dreams like a thug in the night. You see through his eyes; it's a pitiful sight. He gives you some pills; you soon fill strange. You smell flesh burning, people hollering in pain. You pinch yourself as hard as you can; you can't fill anything. You're still human.

You've entered a tunnel full of smoke and skulls; you see half-visible people talking mess doing drugs.

"Am I in hell? "I asked in my mind? I'm only twenty-four. I thought I had more time. My mother goes to church; she doesn't miss a beat. I thought that this would somehow also save me. (A loud voice yelled "No") I want to go back. I wouldn't say I like it here; next, I trembled with cries and tears.

Everything was dead; it had no life; next, pieces of my body started to die; Finally, I asked God for one more chance; I woke up in my bed under a new circumstance.

OLD BONES

These old bones still cry out. I heard the ground say, shut your mouth. They are tired but still can't rest; they've expressed how They're oppressed. Knees on necks taken his wind; he's not with us, what a sin.

Skittles and Ice-tea were going to see his pops; he got ambushed by a want to be Cop. He was told to please stand down; you're not the law; stop following him around just because his skin was brown. So he took out his weapon and took you down.

Taking a nice jog as he did in spare time, murdered by three men, had never crossed his mind! Laying in her bed.

They picked the wrong house; did they investigate correctly, I seriously doubt.' These old bones lay deep beneath the ground; they still can't rest due to the chaos of the sound.

A senseless traffic stop mistakes her taser for her gun; Now, this beautiful mother has to live without her son.

Hands were up high, and he still got shot; he was only a teen; the bones still cry out. Playing in the park, the toy wasn't real. It seems as if you are anxious to draw your steal. Taking a fun walk with his friend by his side. There is no way this young man had to die. Well, the list goes on about these senseless deaths. These are a few, so the bones can't rest!

FRIENDS SPEAK

Oprah Winfrey told Mya Angelo that these girls were wearing their paints too far off their hips. It seems that they can get more respect if they reveal less. Mya Angelo states that the young men are also wearing too low paints. No respect for anyone. Opara says," the world has changed drastically" Mya, I agree. People have become lovers of themselves; they don't fear God, and "don't forget prayer was removed from the schools. Oparah that"explains all the threats, fights, and crimes. We will continue to pray about this subject, Mya Well, some adults show irate behavior. Could this be where our teenagers are learning" it?

Your best friend Gail couldn't have a better friend; she is a gift; she is God sent. I love you, Oprah; that's all I can say. Oprah, I pray for this world and hope it gets better; you hear that gas is over seven dollars? Yes, The taxpayers and all of us who purchase gas are mixed up in a mess we didn't create!

PSALM 91

He that dwelleth in the secret place of the Most High shall abide under the shadow of the Almighty

I will say of the Lord he is my refuge and my fortress: my God in him will I trust. Surely he shall deliver thee from the fowler's snare and the noisome pestilence. He should cover thee with his feathers, and under his wings shall thou trust. His truth shall be thy shield and buckler. Though should not be afraid for thy terror by night; nor the arrow that flieth by day; nor the pestilence that walketh in darkness; nor the destruction that wasteth at noonday. A thousand shall fall at thy side and ten thousand at thy right hand, but it shall not come nigh thee. Only with thine eyes shalt thy behold and see the reward of the wicked. Because thy had made the Lord which is my refuge even the Most High my habitation, they shall bear thee up in their hands lest thou dash a foot against a stone. Thou shalt tread upon the lion and adder; the young lion and dragon shall thy trample under thy feet. Therefore because he has set his love upon me, I will deliver him. I will set him on high; because he hath known my name. He shall call upon me, and I will answer him. I will be with him in trouble; I will deliver and honor him. I will satisfy him and show him my salvation with long life.

JEREMIAH 29:16, 11

For I know the plans I have for you declares the Lord, "plans to prosper you and not to harm you, plans to give you hope and A future. Then you will call on me and come and pray to me, and I will listen to you. Then, you will seek me and find me when you seek me with all your heart, you will find me", declares the Lord.

DAUGHTERS

Daughters are sweet with lots of spice. These are the words that make them nice. They are lovable and enjoyable, too; my heart just wooed when I met you. You light up my world; with sunshine and smiles; you defiantly know how to turn my dials. Daughters are beautiful, like a daisy flying free. God made her, especially for me.

WRONG VIBES

When people feel rejected, it establishes a sense of humiliation, frustration, and aggravation. You never know whom life you may have affected with your vulgar insults. Your vibes need adjusting; see, you are not trusting with yourself. You belittle others to make yourself feel as if you own the world. In all truths, your vibes need to go through a washing cycle. Who am I? It's not important

I keep vibes even and smooth. I don't have time for you to be rude.

Please change it's wrong what you do. So you don't feel the pain you put others through. Your vibes are hurtful; they dig deep I've been watching you for the last few weeks. What if the jokes or laughs were about you? I feel you wouldn't know what to do; please change swift give thoughts to one's feelings.

You can be a better person that can become appealing.

TRIPPIN

I took a trip to that windy city; that mean Chi-Town gets very windy. When that plane rolled on the ground, those gusty winds just knocked me down. I ran fast to catch my hat; I didn't know it would get windy like that. Big shoulders twirl and smack your face. The windy city is quite a place. I met celebrities in my hotel; The Ritz Carlton staff treated me well. The food was terrific everywhere that I dined; the waiters were all so, very kind. The traffic is heavy every day of the week; it's always busy. I didn't get sleep. The sun is beautiful and pleasant on the eyes; plenty of activities when I rise. There are Skyscrapers, Architecture, and Museums to see. Big Shoulders Town is the place to be.

JEWELS & RAGS

I wondered why you thought of me as jewels; you misinterpreted me for rags. Hands down, everybody, no applause. You are the owner of two faces; the one you wear to impress the crowd; you treat me fantastic. The other is wicked and cold as a stone; it's not official when were alone.

Jewels & rags have no comparisons; one's genuine, the others embarrassing. Jewels are shimmers of one's personality. Rags are bags of irrationality, for example, your outburst and attacks. Your rags are so heavy they weigh down my back. You lost your backbone not long after birth. Your senseless and heartless time is not worth the rags you gave me that I thought were jewels. I never thought that a person could be so cruel. So I go without taking anything from you, like the end of my story, we are through!

THE SHUFFLED CARDS

The ace rules the deck. She must be a woman; she's confident, intelligent, and know-how to move throughout the rest of the deck to keep all others in line; next is the King; not many cards can take his place or beat him; he lay down the laws the rest of the deck follow. He is the lion in the jungle; he's usually the final card that makes the difference. The queen answers to no one; she is brilliant, acquisitive, and has powers beyond anyone's belief. Jack is the son of the queen and King; it would be nothing but lethal to bother Jack in any way; in other words, it is better to be his friend, not his enemy. Joker is the killer of the game; he is pretty dangerous; he has no sense of time, feelings, or concepts of anyone's life. You see the joker run as if you're the star on the track field. Two through ten are the gate keepers' soldiers, all the other numbers. Nothing can pass these soldiers unless permitted by the Queen or King. The system of the cards works because every card knows and respects its position.

PHOTOS ON THE WALL

The photos on the wall should be re-range periodically. Don't let them get too comfortable in the same spot for twenty years.

The photos can hear the screams of its ancestors. So mix them up and place them on the wall in another room. Sometimes the pictures whisper out your secrets, although the image caught by the lenses is not the accurate picture that other photos see.

These walls have held scholars, children to adulthood, me, you, and many more before us. Don't be afraid; the walls have also held some criminals' faces that no longer belong in this society. I did not say they couldn't be born again. I'm just saying our walls have been more than busy holding all these pictures. The frames are the various stages that make the photos dance. They stay at the border of the photograph. Sometimes the image looks like it's smiling at me, so I smile back. I suspect that photos will have cameras to record the things people can't see or say in the future. So they are that it may help unsolved cases that go cold.

RESTAURANT ZERO

"Would you eat your dinner with rats?"

I spotted rat droppings on the floor near the kitchen; nevertheless, I know the difference between rat turds and peppercorns! I'm finishing up the last of my dinner. I walked over to the kitchen to advise the waiter that she had forgotten my water. I see a slinky older man with three freckles on each cheek. His pants are saggy; his shirt is dingy white; he has enormous black shoes; the older man strolls; I can see he's tired with little energy. The older man's name tag reads Harvey Kinkel.

Harriet, my waiter's eyes meet mine as she massages and rubs her feet. Harriet quickly jumps to her feet and makes her way to the sink. Harriet takes her bare hands and fills six glasses with ice. I'm in disbelief that Harriet did not wash her hands sense she needed to touch the ice to serve it. I believe Mr. Harvey is making her nervous; in addition, Harriet is all over the place. They were the temporary staff. My eyes do a quick scan of the kitchen. The back door was open for air, although it was about 95 degrees. The screen has a huge hole that allows flies and insects to fly in, and the dishwasher has a sign that emphasizes breaking.

Dishes are piled a mile high in some dirty dishwater; the wall is greasy and dull, and needless to say, no one washes it!

Mr. Harvey comes into the kitchen from outside with a kangaroo on a leash. He rushes to tie the leash on a nail sticking out the wall; next, he came over to the door and advised me I could not be near the kitchen!

Mr. Harvey gives me a little shove back towards the dining area, "I yell, hey, you can't have an animal in the kitchen." I saw the rat turds too!

Harriet rushes past me so fast that she drops a hot pepper out of a bowl of salad; she picks it up with her bare hands and throws it back in the salad. Harriet is the only one working fifteen tables. I can't let her serve that salad or six glasses of water to customers. I know it's a rough night for Mr. Harvey and Harriet; nevertheless, people deserve dignity. I purposely bump into Harriet, causing her to drop everything. I explain to Harriet, and I am so sorry. Harriet's hands go up in the air with Ice water, and salads are everywhere. All of this is making me sick to my stomach. I rush off to the men's room. I hear a customer in the bathroom on the phone saying, the food here is excellent. I will bring you to attend next week"." To think I can't wait to eat here for the first time". I give this restaurant a big fat zero!

Loudly, a commotion outside of the restroom in the restaurant. Several departments of health officers abruptly rushed into the restaurant to advise all employees that the restaurant would be closed down. I'm not surprised; this restaurant failed so many regulations. Although, several letters, in fact, all in all, were ignored by Mr. Kinkle. One of the department head workers seems intrigued, taping signs on the restaurant's glass closed until further notice.

Mr. Harvey is so sad. I hate seeing him this way. He pointed to me and asked that I call his employees in the blue book on the kitchen shelf and advise them the restaurant is being closed down. Next, Mr. Harvey asked that I take the kangaroo. I point out I have no room for an animal of his size, plus I can't take care of him. Finally, Mr. Harvey asked me to take him to the city zoo. "I will miss him, "Mr. Harvey stated with tearful eyes.

I went into the kitchen and sat at a broken-down old desk to call Mr. Harvey's employees. There must be twenty-five employees in this phone book; why are only two people working tonight? I can clearly say that Mr. Harvey let his employees get away with excuses. First, call "hello, can I speak to Mr. Verrado?" this is he." "Mr. Verrado, this is Restaurant zero calling to advise you the restaurant is being closed down, "what, why, where is Mr. Harvey? "He's talking to authorities. "I will come in tomorrow, I promise." Don't bother. "Where is the kangaroo asked, Mr. Verrado"? I will take him to the city zoo. I'm sorry, Mr. Verrado, I have several other employees to call; It all comes down to this. You have to take your next job seriously

DAY AT THE LIBRARY

I don't want to live in this world another day!

My computer is on the bum again, so I am going to the library. "EEK" I forget my flash drive.

It seems as if I'm going to have a bad day. I scan the room suspiciously; as a matter of fact, it's hot, crowded, and noisy." What" is it! Children's day or something? I thought to myself. Where are the children's parents? Then "Bam"! "There goes a small bookshelf with books and flyers "falling everywhere." The bookshelf almost fell on one of the children in seconds.

The Liberian zooms over to ensure none of the boys are hurt; she escorts the three boys back to their seats. She examined the room; her expression said, where are the children's parents? At the desk across from me, I keep hearing this knocking sound. "Is this happening? This man is knocking on the table abruptly and making sucking sounds with his mouth as if trying to make a rap song. "Hello, sir, this is a library." I did not say that out loud; however, I sure wanted to.

Who bought their kids here to chase each other all over the place. I'm looking behind the counter where three people are working! No one is saying anything. I believe they are afraid to say something to the parents whom, by the way, are nowhere to be found." O, no, there is one seat left, and it looks like the loud lady is coming right towards me to sit down. Did I mention she is on her phone arguing with it? Sounds like her boyfriend? This lady has used every unpleasant word in the book." I finally screamed out loud." "This is a library, not a place to be rude." No one is respecting no one here! (Lady on the phone)." You better not hang up on me." Hello, hello, are you there". The lady hollers out. He hung up on me. Finally, a worker asked the lady to silence her cell phone. The lady's shoulders rose, the head went back slightly to the side, eyes looking over her glasses. Mouth poked out. She "looked at the librarian," I thought she would hit" her.

The Weasley man working behind the counter did not come over to say anything!

The lady hollered at the librarian with the loudest words ever! He's lucky my phone is dead! I'm going to kick his. Well, you know the rest.

The two little kids chasing each other in the library (sister and brother), their mother just bought them each a happy meal; this made them a little quieter; at the same time. The "huge sign on the wall clearly states, "No Eating in the Library, lady." That's it! I had to go to the counter and say something. I told the guard I; couldn't concentrate; there was too much noise in this library. Do you see the kids that were chasing each other eating their McDonalds? The sign states no eating in here. Why won't you say anything to their parents? The (Guard) replied that they don't listen to us and want to argue. I asked, why don't you call the police to assist you? The guard explained; that the last time I called the police; my car ended up with pink and purple paint. You're kidding. I'm not, and I could not press charges because the camera did not pick up who did this.

You know I've seen better days than this. No one, including the children, is following the library's rules; This opens the door for disrespect to each other. This world we live in isn't perfect; however, what kind of world would this be; if we did not have rules? We would be living in the wild, wild west. I have been in the library for less than forty-five minutes, and at least seven major written rules seem to be invisible.

Liberians are afraid to do their job because of retaliation; The children are too young to understand you don't run, chasing each other in the library. The parents left the children there to purchase their happy meal. The lady is arguing with her boyfriend, "come on," she knows better! I can honestly speak for myself and a few others in the library. We do not care to hear your conversation with your boyfriend. You are rude to speak it out loud and not be courtesy of others.

The man is hitting on the table, making strange loud sounds from his mouth; there are no books in front of him or paperwork." Why is he even here? This is not an audition for a contest; take that somewhere else. I gave him the "worst look, and it did not even bother him. I don't want to live in this world another day without making a difference.

I'm not going to complain anymore to the staff that is on. I'm simply going to go to a different library. My plan to make this problem better is to write the state governor and explain why all libraries should have trained security guards. But, before I write the governor, I would like to do a little experiment, which would include me going to at least four other libraries and taking notes on the behavior of the other staff and people in the library. Hopefully, this will change disrespectful people coming into the library, treating it as a social club or daycare.

It goes on for an hour, and the children's parents "Wait, guess who just arrived here? The parents. I don't know. I must wear my feelings on my face because here comes the boy's mother right towards me.

I know I'm a stranger to you; I need to ask you a huge favor. I pointed to myself. "Yes," you. "Can you please give me a ride to this job interview I have in thirty minutes? My boyfriend won't take me, and I need this job. I asked where the children will go while you're inside interviewing? That is the second part of the favor I wanted to ask you." Can they sit in the car with you for a few minutes? I don't know? We don't know each other." Hello, my name is Tabatha; I have four sons I'm trying to feed. What is your name? I'm Sallyanne. "Pleased to meet you, Sallyanne. "Can you please" do me this favor.? "There's no one else you can ask? "No. We'll come all right! Hopefully, the children are tired from all that running they did when you were gone. Tabetha, yes, the children will most likely go to sleep. Thank you so much. "I'll say it here for the last time. I don't want to live in this world another day and not make a difference".

THE EXPERIMENT

I dressed very poorly and went into a restaurant in Amherst; I will not mention the name.

I went over to the counter; so I would be seated, a group of people dashed in front of me, skipping me.

In conclusion, the waitress ushered them to their table. I sighed while making a few noises and letting them know that this was unacceptable.

I witnessed that no one wanted to seat me or talk to me because they thought I was a bum. I had cut-off pants, a torn, raggedy shirt, mixed match socks, one purple and one orange. My hair looked terrible; my coat was too small and grimy. Finally, I asked, can I be seated, please? The waitress stated, we'll be right with you. I eased out the door after watching several other people being seated.

After going home for a few hours; then, I returned to the restaurant. I look fantastic to make a statement, from head to toe. I had on all name-brand clothing; I had an expensive Chanel handbag on my arm none of the waiters had a clue that I was that bum that left a few hours ago. This time the service was out of sight. Being that it may, I was seated immediately. I even skipped three people that were already waiting.

The gestures and expressions of the people waiting did not surprise me; they were not happy and felt this was not fair.

The waitress, I had her name tag, Shavonn; she poured me a sample of cabaret it filled half the glass.

At another table, a woman sitting across from me whispered, "You didn't pour me that much in my sample. The waiter just ignored her

She went to the back where the food was getting cooked. I watched as a few employees gathered; on the contrary, an employee asked me, "Is that a real Chanel bag"? I spoke as if I was not from this part of town. I stated with a British accent, "why sure, it's natural I wouldn't get caught Alive with a fake handbag; meanwhile, I hear a different employee state you shouldn't ask her that. After eating, I left my waiter an eight-dollar tip. From the look on her face, she expected more. The moral of this story is to treat everyone the same. As a person who appeared not to have very much, I couldn't get any service. A Few hours later, the workers circled me as if I was a dolphin in the water. What if the bum was an angel?

(VILLANELLE) LOVE WARMTH SOUL

You spoke of a love that is present and past.
Our love came from tears and pain.
One for all because all for one.

In a flash of a moment, our love would not last
I still love you despite the stain.
The memories and years were so much fun.

You were most bitter alone in a class
I, too, will accept some of the blame.
One for all and all for one

Eating cheese with wine and enjoying the smooth sound of jazz.
Our love was sweet in the rain
The memories and years were lots of fun.

I was your soldier but withered like grass.
I felt the hurt in my veins
One for all and all for one

Our love was different, like a fumeless gas.
It was forceful, like the speed of a train.
The memories and years were defiantly fun.
One for all because all for one.

STARRY NIGHT OVER THE RHONE

Let not your eyes blink with worry and heights
Mysterious visions of this stary night.
Glimmers shape beauty near and far.
You can reach out and touch a star. Explosions relieve colors
From Van Gogh's name. Starry night rhone makes handsome the
frame.
Streaks of visions surround mother earth. Starry Night Rhone
contributes to birth.
The brightness, the essence, brings forth love.
Nights over Rhone is, saluting Starry Night above.

LET THERE BE LIGHT

Let there be light because of the dark there scared—a boy with his dog trembles with fear.

There are no batteries or flashlights near. Their eyes are glowing began to tear.

There are strange sounds from the whistling of the thunder.

Will the storm cease? I certainly wonder. Rain and hail hit the window's shutters.

A boy with his dog hides under the covers.

"Bam," the door slams dad is home. The boy and the dog are no longer alone.

The boy is happy. The dog grabs his bone

Let there be light in this peaceful, sweet home. "Suddenly," the lights come back on.

HE ROSE AGAIN

They hung him high as they pierced his soul—no remorse for man.

The clouds turned cold in the sky as they stabbed his feet and hands.

One drop of blood, minds grew weary; they couldn't change what they'd done. Somewhere in the of Romans jealously;

They've killed our father's son. A mother helpless cries out in pain as her son's life leaves the earth. All the believers show sorrow; the Romans have no self-worth. The Romans laugh as they sit on their horses to temp the son of God. When his head dropped, the Romans assumed it was a final nod. "Suddenly," the rain, the winds, and the sky grew dark while the wind blew out of control. The Romans trembled at their actions. My father took control. They were most frightened as they rode off; they didn't look back again. One of the Romans hollered was the son of man?

Three days later, in the cave, the stone was rolled away. The body of Christ has risen; this is resurrection day!

ESCAPED HEARTS

Jealous envy is best buddies; they come to cause you significant discomfort. His job is to cause you humiliation beyond reasonable measures. She made several attempts to reconcile with you; her world stirs as unwanted voices giggle to raise her pain levels. He is almost there to a boiling level. Looking right and left, there is no escape. He escalates to invite others in now that you are the center of attention. No one should ever feel this unacceptable humiliation. He has dreamed one hundred dreams to make this all stop. It's like that feeling of falling, and right before you hit bottom, you wake up in a cold sweat. Now she's trying to decipher between reality and a horrible nightmare. This humiliation has three levels; I pray that she never experiences the third level. That level will set her free in a different place and time. See, you have to trade your thoughts while nearly sacrificing it all. Incomparable is what it is. You wait and beg for revenge. Being that it may, it's not happening fast enough. Keep your dignity and you're strength. These two buddies will carry you through.

YESTER YEARS

I am old but once was young. Memories bring back so much fun.

I laugh, but then I cry; some memories get trapped inside.

I will name these yesteryears A life that brings smiles; and tears.

I struggle and hope to remember; that part of my mind I had to surrender. It comes and goes

Whenever it likes, it's sort of like an ongoing fight. I have a daughter and also a son; yesteryears are not over

They've just begun.

(SONNET) LOVE B

Is it not of me to be selfish?
Great love only works when you try.
You make excuses. You're helpless.
I spent many hours trying to get by.
Sunrises are beautiful but not all alone.
You must be new to this; it's ok.
When it's dusk, the darkest hour I, Rome.
Our friendship is too much work I may not stay.
Butterflies communicate; their spots never change.
You are not in this alone.
You try, then you quit; this is strange.
We agreed to make a happy home
Maybe we can scrap this, then try our love again.
Sour search our hearts; it lies deep within.

(SONNET) BY MOUTH

When women of race make a statement.
The world asks the question of why.
Their boots are uncomfortable on this pavement.
The blisters on my feet make me cry.
Choirs sing cords while birds sing songs.
Hold your hand up if you've ever been wrong.
Twist of faith holds up my pen.
Hollering loud to; do not sin.
Reinstatement gives a cleansed new soul.
Live in this world that's careless and cold.
Women make statements as successful as men
Walking proudly with high heels, hold up your chin.
They understood then all worked out.
Please pass it on; it's a word by mouth.

BLAZE CHAISE

Ghetto boys fly
Point in the eye.
Look at the sky.
We real tough.
We get rough.
We talk stuff.
We sing praise
We get raise
We rephrase blase

(VILLANELLE) THE TENANT

The woman upstairs is suspicious.
Vistors go up there but never come down.
Some may think I'm ridiculous.

She watches movies that are superstitious
The visitors are too quiet; they don't make a sound.
The woman upstairs is suspicious.

The food she prepares smells delicious.
After eating, the guests are never around.
Some may think I'm ridiculous.

I know she cooks nutritious.
I pray the next guest "does not" back down.
The woman upstairs is suspicious.

The woman upstairs is viscous.
I wonder if her guest is from this town?
Some might say I'm ridiculous.

I hope she realizes I'm hip-to-this.
Guest go up and never come down.
The woman upstairs is viscous.
She's sneaky, plus suspicion

STAR STRUCK

Wide hips with perfect lips. Shoulders tall, waist is small.

Lashes are inviting; she's that exciting.

Confident and sure she's far from bored, you'll adore and want her more. She's lovely and Intriguing; conversation is receiving. She is accepted by the majority. What gives her this kind of authority? Is it the

hype, the people, and the fame? It no longer excites her; it's all a shame.

She is starstruck and can't love a soul. Her attitude is awful; her heart is cold. But unfortunately, the world covers up the truth to be told.

They Conceal the boundary and then treat her like gold. She 's no fool; she lives to survive people that know her claims she connives and deprives. Most don't believe them because she won't let you get close; her guard is up she stands her post. She is Starstruck and can care less if you agree. Starstruck is the title that set her free.

FUNCTIONS

Dysfunctional, dismayed, thinking of the time when actuality speaks the truth.

You don't like me, and I don't like you.

I can call me black, however, if you say it. It lacks.
I can call myself white; nevertheless, if you say it's not right

Two different races in two unlike communities; Some have none or more opportunities.
Gay and transgender people are a part of this.
It's none of your business what their sexual choice is

Dysfunctional, dismayed, thinking of a time that the reset button gets pushed now.
I wanted to push the button forty years ago.

Bragging on someone else money won't buy you that house you keep passing off the threw way. Steve Harvey just bought Tyler Perrys' castle.
Now that is some accomplishment. Congrats to you both.

To all the hip, shakers; the moneymakers, and the money takers. I know they're in every race.
Not all people are bad, but they disgrace every race. So how could you point your finger to call me dysfunctional?

What gets me is that you are entirely comfortable.

Are there some Bill Cobsys that haven't gotten caught? I mean, did Reynhard Sinaga use date rape drugs to assault men?

Why are drugs such as this even sold? The pharmaceutical doesn't know they do what there told.

Is this the truth or a bunch of vicious lies? This misery goes past a needle in the eye. Emmit Tills' mother had a right to cry. I'm exhausted from this because

All lives matter. They were supposed to be climbing yet, were falling down the ladder. We have knees on necks, whips on trees, the body's being lynched. God help us, please. Things are messed up and out of control. So did Jussie Smollett have whispers of lies that he told? Should we believe him ? the evidence shows the truth. Why in the world would you do what you do? Consequences are brutal; they always come back; they turn full circle and fall in your lap.

GOD IS COMING BACK

God's recollect of us is disappointing.

    He gave us his son; we ruined the anointing. Brother against brother, a daughter against mother

    This foolishness wouldn't happen if you genuinely love her.

    God is coming back; you better be ready!

    God is coming back; you better tell your family

    With all power in his hands. God has a plan.

    Are you ready, or is your head in the sand?

    God is waiting to forgive your sin.

    You need to trust him so he can fulfill his plan.

HOPE

H ls for "help." We're asking God to take us out of this hell

O is for overall. Were all suffering in some form, some people in silence?
The beginning of self-destruction looks like this.

P is for pain, which switched places with progress now were right back
to hurt' sharp, aching, throbbing senseless deaths

E is for effective change that must happen before it's too late.

Hope

H is for " Hollering." As loud as I can. Do you hear me?

O is for overwhelmed. Were all feeling overload right about now?

P is for patience; we will pray and wait; then pray and wait for some
more. Most of us know who's we are.

E is for an effort to come to an understanding that shall help us all, or
will it be egoistic brainstorming that has destroyed and drained life?

Boastful, opinionated, selfish verses, we have faith.

MARQUIS
Who'sWho®

August 6, 2021

Dear Sonya Daniels-Hines,

It is with great pleasure that we welcome you to our prestigious roster of Albert Nelson Marquis Lifetime Achievement inductees. We feel that your extensive experience and notable accomplishments make you truly deserving of this prominent award.

In order to recognize your distinction appropriately, we will feature your new Lifetime Achievement honor in our flagship hardcover registry, Who's Who in America.

Please rest assured that our team of specialists is always here to assist you. You may contact us by phone at ██████ ████████.

Congratulations once again on being chosen as an Albert Nelson Marquis Lifetime Achievement inductee. We are honored to recognize you among others in your field and within the Marquis Who's Who organization.

Sincerely,

The Marquis Who's Who Editorial Team

THE MARQUIS WHO'S WHO
PUBLICATIONS BOARD

is pleased to recognize

SONYA DANIELS-HINES

as a recipient of the

Albert Nelson Marquis Lifetime Achievement Award

an honor reserved for Marquis Biographees
who have achieved career longevity
and demonstrated unwavering excellence
in their chosen fields.

2021

ABOUT THE AUTHOR

Sonya Daniels/Hines Greek/English Her name means beautiful, wisdom. Sonya is ambitious as she writes her way through life. Her love of writing is exceptional. Sonya writes Fiction, and non-fiction is her favorite form of writing. Her hobbies include arts and crafts, music, cooking, and writing.

www.ingramcontent.com/pod-product-compliance
Lightning Source LLC
Chambersburg PA
CBHW031219120626
46545CB00003B/910